MY CRICKET BOOK OF MOTHER GOOSE

Illustrated by Tim & Greg Hildebrandt

Platt & Munk, Publishers · New York
A division of Grosset & Dunlap

Copyright © 1987, 1972 by Platt & Munk, Publishers, a division of Grosset & Dunlap, a member of The Putnam Publishing Group, New York. All rights reserved. Published simultaneously in Canada. Printed in Singapore. ISBN 0-448-46536-1   A B C D E F G H I J

This material previously published in
Mother Goose, A Treasury of Best-Loved Rhymes

LITTLE BOY BLUE

Little Boy Blue,
Come blow your horn,
The sheep's in the meadow,
The cow's in the corn.
But where is the little boy
Who looks after the sheep?
He's under the haystack,
Fast asleep.
Will you wake him?
No, not I!
For if I do,
He's sure to cry.

HARK, HARK,
THE DOGS DO BARK

Hark, hark, the dogs do bark!
The beggars are coming to town.
Some in rags and some in tags,
And some in velvet gowns.

YANKEE DOODLE

Yankee Doodle went to town,
Riding on a pony.
Stuck a feather in his hat
And called it macaroni.

DAFFY-DOWN-DILLY

Daffy-Down-Dilly
Has come up to town
In a yellow petticoat
And a green gown.

THE MUFFIN MAN

"Oh, do you know the muffin man,
The muffin man, the muffin man,
Oh, do you know the muffin man,
Who lives in Drury Lane?"
"Oh yes, I know the muffin man,
The muffin man, the muffin man,
Oh yes, I know the muffin man
Who lives in Drury Lane."

LITTLE JACK HORNER

Little Jack Horner
Sat in a corner,
Eating his Christmas pie.
He put in his thumb
And pulled out a plum,
And said,
    "What a good boy am I!"

OLD MOTHER HUBBARD

Old Mother Hubbard
Went to the cupboard
To get her poor dog a bone,
But when she got there
The cupboard was bare,
And so the poor dog had none.

JACK SPRAT

Jack Sprat could eat no fat,
His wife could eat no lean,
And so, between the two of them,
They licked the platter clean.

RABBIT, RABBIT,
CARROT-EATER

Rabbit, Rabbit, carrot-eater,
Says he, "There is nothing sweeter
Than a carrot every day—
Munch and crunch
    and run away."

PETER PIPER

Peter Piper picked
A peck of pickled peppers,
A peck of pickled peppers
Peter Piper picked.
If Peter Piper picked
A peck of pickled peppers,
Where's the peck of pickled
    peppers
Peter Piper picked?

PETER, PETER, PUMPKIN-EATER

Peter, Peter, pumpkin-eater,
Had a wife and couldn't keep her.
He put her in a pumpkin shell
And there he kept her very well.

JACK AND JILL

Jack and Jill went up the hill
To fetch a pail of water,
Jack fell down
And broke his crown,
And Jill came tumbling after.

THERE WAS
AN OLD WOMAN
LIVED UNDER A HILL

There was an old woman
Lived under a hill,
And if she's not gone
She lives there still.

HUMPTY DUMPTY

Humpty Dumpty sat on a wall,
Humpty Dumpty had a great fall.
All the king's horses
And all the king's men
Couldn't put Humpty together again.

LITTLE MISS MUFFET

Little Miss Muffet
Sat on a tuffet,
Eating her curds and whey.
Along came a spider
Who sat down beside her,
And frightened
 Miss Muffet away.

MARY HAD A LITTLE LAMB

Mary had a little lamb,
Its fleece was white as snow,
And everywhere that Mary went
The lamb was sure to go.
He followed her to school one day,
Which was against the rule.
It made the children laugh and play
To see a lamb at school.

LITTLE BO PEEP

Little Bo Peep has lost her sheep
And can't tell where to find them.
Leave them alone, and they'll come home,
Wagging their tails behind them.

THERE WAS A CROOKED MAN

There was a crooked man
Who walked a crooked mile,
He found a crooked sixpence
Against a crooked stile.
He bought a crooked cat,
Which caught a crooked mouse,
And they all lived together
In a little crooked house.

THERE WAS AN OLD WOMAN
WHO LIVED IN A SHOE

There was an old woman
Who lived in a shoe,
She had so many children
She didn't know what to do.
She gave them some broth
Without any bread,
And spanked them all soundly
And sent them to bed.

PEASE-PORRIDGE HOT

Pease-porridge hot,
Pease-porridge cold,
Pease-porridge in the pot,
Nine days old.
Some like it hot,
Some like it cold,
Some like it in the pot,
Nine days old.

JACK BE NIMBLE

Jack be nimble,
Jack be quick,
Jack jump over
the candlestick.

HICKORY, DICKORY, DOCK

Hickory, dickory, dock,
The mouse ran up the clock!
The clock struck one
And down he ran,
Hickory, dickory, dock.

DIDDLE, DIDDLE,
DUMPLING

Diddle, diddle, dumpling,
My son John,
Went to bed
With his stockings on—
One shoe off
And one shoe on—
Diddle, diddle, dumpling,
My son John.

RUB-A-DUB-DUB

Rub-a-dub-dub,
Three men in a tub,
And who do you think they be?
The butcher, the baker,
The candlestick maker,
Turn them out, knaves all three.

STAR LIGHT, STAR BRIGHT

Star light, star bright,
First star I see tonight,
I wish I may, I wish I might,
Have the wish I wish tonight.

HEY DIDDLE DIDDLE

Hey! diddle, diddle!
The cat and the fiddle,
The cow jumped over the moon.
The little dog laughed
To see such sport,
And the dish ran away with the spoon.